Stephen Tossy

HOW TO OFFEND GOD
AND SUFFER THE CONSEQUENCES
IN SEVEN EASY LESSONS

Brother Gysa Dime

Also by Brother Cysa Dime:

When All Else Fails, Read the Directions
or
How to Study the Bible

HOW TO OFFEND GOD
AND SUFFER THE CONSEQUENCES
IN SEVEN EASY LESSONS

—Or—

THE SEVEN DEADLY SINS

A BIBLE STUDY
BY
BROTHER CYSA DIME

HighWay
A division of Anomalos Publishing House
Crane

HighWay
A division of Anomalos Publishing House, Crane 65633
© 2009 by Brother Cysa Dime
All rights reserved. Published 2009
Printed in the United States of America

09   1

ISBN-10: 0982323549 (cloth)
EAN-13: 9780982323540 (cloth)
A CIP catalog record for this book is available from the Library of Congress.

Cover illustration and design by Patty Findley
Unless otherwise noted, Scripture taken from the NEW AMERICAN
STANDARD BIBLE®, Copyright© 1960, 1962, 1963, 1968, 1971, 1972,
1973, 1975, 1977, 1995 by The Lockman Foundation. Used by permission.

Definitions of original language words indicated by Strong's numbers
are from:

Old Testament:
The Complete Word Study Dictionary: Old Testament
Copyright 2005. AMG Publishers. Edited by Gene Carpenter &
Warren Baker

New Testament:
The Complete Word Study Dictionary: New Testament
Copyright 1993. AMG International. Edited by Spiros Zodhiates &
Warren Baker

Each is used by permission.

The "virtues" attributed to Geoffrey Chaucer are from "The Parson's Tale,"
from *The Canterbury Tales*.

All quotes by Matthew Henry are from his six-volume commentary on
the whole Bible.

The italicized words in Scripture were formatted as such by the Bible
translators to indicate added words that are not in the original Greek,
Hebrew, and other original language words.

CONTENTS

PREFACE

I BELIEVE THAT just about everyone has a piece of the puzzle. If you have spent your entire life in one denomination, especially one local congregation under one pastor, you will find some things in this book that you may have never thought about before. Do not be surprised if you are halted in your tracks here and there.

The famous poem, *To a Louse*, by Robert Burns about a woman strutting around with her new hat, not knowing that it had lice, ends with:

> O wad some Power the giftie gie us
> To see oursels as ithers see us!

1

Hopefully, this book will allow you to see yourself as God sees you and realize how frequently you commit all of the Seven Deadly Sins. I pray that this motivates you to ask forgiveness and take corrective actions.

I have something in common with St. Paul. I come across in writing much more fiercely and authoritatively than I really am in person. Do not get put off by this.

INTRODUCTION

THIS BOOK IS a follow-up of my previous book, *When All Else Fails, Read the Directions, or How to Study the Bible*. In this "sins book" the reader can, as it were, "look over my shoulder" and see how I apply the analytical methods described in the study book. The reader is encouraged to use these methods to expand on what I have written for their own practice and benefit. Read large chunks of Scripture around the passages I present. Look up the original language words using Strong's numbers. Consult the *Treasury of Scripture Knowledge* for cross-references. Once you come to your own conclusions, consult commentaries for a sanity check.

BACKGROUND

In the early days of Christianity, church leaders noticed certain sins that were commonly committed by the laypeople; who thought that because they were not prohibited by secular laws, they were unimportant. These sins have disastrous consequences. They were codified as the Seven Deadly Sins. Unfortunately, everyone, including church officials, commits all seven of them to some extents.

They will damage your soul and are an act of impoliteness to God. All of them will damage your body in some way. An example is gluttony, which will produce obesity and hasten the onset of diabetes, heart disease, and some forms of cancer. I have seen many people suffer premature death from this.

These sins are not just prohibited by the church; they are also condemned by secular authorities. For example, gluttony was called a moral vice by the ancient Greek philosophers. Today, psychiatrists call it the mental illness of eating disabilities. Medicine calls the results of gluttony the disease of obesity.

You can get a good handle on your relationship with God by your reaction to learning about sins. If you are concerned about how you have disobeyed God, you know Him well. If you make excuses about why you commit these sins or why they are not sins, you do not know God very well or not at all. Hiding your head in the sand and ignoring these sins, will not prevent you from suffering the spiritual consequences from committing them.

You can use the knowledge of these sins to spot fake pastors who are in it for the cushy lifestyle. Do they point out to members in the congregation that they are committing these sins? Do they commit the sins themselves?

I have spent the last forty years in engineering. This has given me experience in observing clues and solving problems. The title about offending God is my reminder about the seriousness of these sins.

In order to help you learn, there are many examples and some exercises. I have included illustrations from the lovable eccentricities of my colorful relatives and others. The purpose of these illustrations is not to be disrespectful to anyone, but to provide easy-to-remember examples that will remind you of the points presented. In this book, I use the general term "God" for members of the Trinity, individually and in different combinations.

ORGANIZATION OF THE BOOK

CHAPTER 1: GLUTTONY: This involves more than eating habits.

CHAPTER 2: PRIDE: This takes many forms, some of them admired by society.

CHAPTER 3: LUST: This involves much more than sexual desires.

CHAPTER 4: WRATH: This is commonly triggered by the act of committing one of the other sins and being frustrated.

CHAPTER 5: AVARICE: This is wanting more than others have.

CHAPTER 6: ENVY: This is the inverse of avarice. You want others to have less, even if you have to take measures to help this occur.

CHAPTER 7: SLOTH. This produces poverty.

FINAL THOUGHTS: This is where I do a wrap-up.

Chapters one through seven describe the sins, give the Scripture basis for it, and suggest ways to avoid or minimize your committing them. I hope you find these suggestions helpful in overcoming these sins. Since this is a Bible study, there are vast amounts of Scripture. The main verses are printed out in full to save time for the reader in not having to look up the references during the first reading.

Each of these chapters start with dictionary definitions. First is the English language word for the sin, which is followed by the definition of some of the original language words for these sins. Over a hundred years ago, Rev. Strong developed a numbering system for the original Hebrew, Greek and other language words used in the Bible. This way laypeople, who did not recognize the unusual alphabets in these languages, could benefit from understanding the meanings of original words underlying the English words in their Bibles. He published Bibles with these numbers superscripted to the English words. He also published a dictionary with the words in numerical order. At the end of each chapter is a list of additional Scripture passages. Once you finish a first reading of this book, you can do additional study by reading these passages.

There are quotations from Matthew Henry (1662–1714), a pastor who wrote a famous six-volume commentary on the whole Bible. It is still in print. Be aware that back then "meat" was the general term for food and "flesh" was the restrictive term for what we today call "meat."

ADDITIONAL READING

There are four older books that I recommend on this subject. One is *The Canterbury Tales* by Geof-frey Chaucer, 1350. Be sure to get a printing with *The Parson's Tale* in full (50+ pages). It is this tale that describes the Seven Deadly Sins. Another book is *Creed or Chaos?* by Dorothy L. Sayers, 1949. There is one chapter on these sins. The whole book is worth reading. You may find these on internet used book search engines, such as bookfinder.com and bibliofind.com. *The Screwtape Letters* by C. S. Lewis has a few pages on gluttony and so does *Mere Christianity*. Both of these books are worth reading cover to cover. It was the reading of these books several times over the years that inspired me to write this book. They probably colored my presentation.

Exercise 1. Now that you know the names of the Seven Deadly Sins write a short paragraph describing each and give examples. As you read each chapter, compare your paragraph with the discussions I present.

GLUTTONY
(GULA)

GLUT'TONY, n. Excess in eating; extravagant indulgence of the appetite for food.

1. Luxury of the table.

2. Voracity of appetite.

—Noah Webster's 1828 Dictionary of American English

H2151 A verb meaning to be vile, frivolous, gluttonous, worthless; to despise. It describes an especially serious corruption of character in a worthless, gluttonous son, closely akin to one who drinks too much. It means to hold up to disdain, to despise.

G5314 A glutton, an excessive or intemperate eater.

(If you do not recognize the G and H numbers, go back to the introduction and read the part about Strong's numbers.)

SUMMARY

Gluttony is an excess. It is used in the phrase "Glut on the market." Temperance is the virtue of not committing this sin. Some of our forefathers considered this the worst of the seven, because people who start out doing this were more likely to commit other sins, especially sloth and lust. Gluttony takes different forms. The most common form of gluttony is an excess in the quantity of food and drink, producing excess body weight or drunkenness if aggressively done over long periods of time.

Gluttony also includes excesses in quality. Some people are proud of this and call themselves epicureans, gourmets, or connoisseurs. Gluttony includes food, clothing, shelter, and transportation far in excess of real needs. I have seen situations where a person has a technology consumer product that is so complex they cannot use it properly, and end up with the functionality of a much cheaper, simpler product.

I am amused by some fake churches, which will not allow membership to people who ruin their health with tobacco products and drink, but accept people who ruin their health with obesity. Another way to spot fake churches is by nepotism. There are "pastors" and other salaried officials with no formal training, such as going to seminary, that are relatives of a pastor who has gone to seminary or some other official. In the church my late mother attended, the head deacon had a nephew who was so inept that he could not get a commercial job. He was made a pastor with disastrous consequences. As far as I know, he was never removed from office.

SCRIPTURE ON GLUTTONY

Gluttony is condemned in many Scriptures:

Deuteronomy 21:19: Then his father and mother shall seize him, and bring him out to the elders of his city at the gateway of his hometown.

20 They shall say to the elders of his city, "This son of ours is stubborn and rebellious, he will not obey us, he is a glutton and a drunkard."

21 Then all the men of his city shall stone him to death; so you shall remove the evil from your midst, and all Israel will hear *of it* and fear.

Both gluttony and juvenile delinquency were capitol offenses under the Old Covenant. The execution was done by the judicial system and not private individuals.

Philippians 3:18: (For many walk, of whom I have told you often, and now tell you even weeping, *that they are* the enemies of the cross of Christ:

19 Whose end *is* destruction, whose God *is their* belly, and *whose* glory is in their shame, who mind earthly things.) (KJV)

Matthew Henry has these comments:

He gives us the characters of those who were the enemies of the cross of Christ. Whose God is their belly. They minded nothing but their sensual appetites. A wretched idol it is, and a scandal for any, but especially for Christians, to sacrifice the favour of God, the peace of their conscience, and their eternal happiness to it. Gluttons and drunkards make a god of their belly, and all their care is to please it and make provision for it. The same observance which good people give to God epicures give to their appetites. Of such he says, "They serve not the Lord Jesus Christ, but their own bellies" (Romans 16:18).

1 Corinthians 6:9: Or do you not know that the unrighteous will not inherit the kingdom of God? Do not be deceived; neither fornicators, nor idolaters, nor adulterers, nor effeminate, nor homosexuals,

10 nor thieves, nor the covetous, nor drunkards, nor revilers, nor swindlers, will inherit the kingdom of God.

Paul shows that this form of gluttony will bar people from heaven.

RESULTS OF GLUTTONY

Proverbs 21:17: He who loves pleasure *will become* a poor man; He who loves wine and oil will not become rich.
Proverbs 23:21: For the heavy drinker and the glutton will come to poverty, and drowsiness will clothe *one* with rags.

Matthew Henry has these comments:

Some particular cautions against those sins which are, of all sins, the most destructive to the seeds of wisdom and grace in the soul, which impoverish and ruin it. Gluttony and drunkenness, Proverbs 23:20, Proverbs 23:21. The world is full of examples of this sin and temptations to it, which all young people are concerned to stand upon their guard against and keep at a distance from *Be not a wine-bibber*; we are allowed to drink *a little wine* (1 Timothy 5:23), but not much, not to make a trade of it, never to drink to excess. *Be not a riotous eater of flesh*, as the Israelites were, who lusted exceedingly after it, saying, *Who will give us flesh to eat*? Whereas Paul, though he is free to eat flesh, yet resolves that *he will eat no flesh while the world stands rather than make his brother to offend*; so indifferent is he to it, 1 Corinthians 8:13. *Be not an* excessive *eater of flesh*. Intemperance must be avoided in meat as well as drink. *Be not a* luxurious *eater of flesh*, not pleased with any thing but what is very nice and delicate, savoury dishes, and forced meat. Some take not only a pleasure, but a pride, in being curious about their diet, and, as they call it, eating well; as if that were the ornament of a gentleman, which is really the shame of a Christian, making a God of the belly.

ADVICE FROM CHAUCER

Chaucer reminds us that there are many externally visible clues to gluttony beyond drunkenness and excess body weight:

Devouring food.
Eating great quantities of food.
Eating before the allotted time.
Immoderate fastidiousness in dressing up
    the food.
Eating greedily.

These remind me of the rhetorical question, "Do you eat to live or live to eat?"

CURES FOR GLUTTONY

As in all sins, the first step is to admit doing them and not make excuses about why you are exempt or what you do is in some way not involved in the sin. In the case of food gluttony, I have heard many excuses. One amusing excuse is that eating certain "healthy" foods in excess is not gluttony; another is that eating to excess keeps your stomach from growling at work and offending customers. The most outrageous excuse was that of a woman who was getting back at her elderly mother for having the audacity to die from some disease of old age. Excuses for the nonfood type involve claiming that someone of their social status is expected to own the items.

My late mother would eat a pint of extra butterfat ice cream each day and think that following it with a diet soda would cancel the effects of the cholesterol and calories in the ice cream. I understand that this is quite common.

Reduce your temptations by not getting near places that sell food (other than grocery stores). Go to the grocery store when you are not hungry and only have mundane foods to eat at home. This means no candy, chocolate, cookies, cakes, pies, pastries or ice cream, and very little meat.

Each time you are tempted to eat when you are

not hungry, ask yourself why. The relief of boredom and anxiety are common triggers. You should relieve these stresses in other ways, such as starting a reading program to fill in your idle time, going for a walk, or finding the cause of your anxiety and treating it at the source.

Memorize some of these Scriptures and repeat them to yourself when you are tempted. Print some out and post them on the refrigerator door. In your daily prayers, mention this problem.

I have found the following rules useful:

- Only eat when you are hungry and not because the clock shows a certain time.
- Eat small quantities and wait a half hour to see if you are still hungry.
- Do not eat within two hours of going to bed no matter how hungry you are. You will wake up not hungry.
- Only eat mundane foods such as fruit and vegetables with no sauces, cooked in the microwave oven.

- Remember that you are only losing weight when it hurts. Remember the saying, "No pain—no gain."

In the case of nonfood gluttony, ask yourself why you want the item. Are you going to use it frequently and all of the features? In my case, I do not buy a new gismo until the old one fails and the repair cost is higher than the price of a new one.

PRACTICE THE VIRTUES OF

Temperance
    2 Peter 1:5: Now for this very reason also, applying all diligence, in your faith supply moral excellence, and in *your* moral excellence, knowledge,
    6 and in *your* knowledge, self-control, and in *your* self-control, perseverance, and in *your* perseverance, godliness,
    7 and in *your* godliness, brotherly kindness, and in *your* brotherly kindness, love.

Moderation
> **Philippians 4:5:** Let your moderation be known unto all men. The Lord is at hand. (KJV)

Abstinence
AB'STINENCE, n. [L. abstinentia. See Abstain.]
1. In general, the act or practice of voluntarily refraining from, or forbearing any action. Abstinence from every thing which can be deemed labor.

More appropriately:
2. The refraining from an indulgence of appetite, or from customary gratifications of animal propensities. It denotes a total forbearance, as in fasting, or a forbearance of the usual quantity. In the latter sense, it may coincide with temperance, but in general, it denotes a more sparing use of enjoyments than temperance. Besides, abstinence implies previous free indulgence; temperance does not.

—Noah Webster's 1828 Dictionary of American English

Sufficiency
> **Proverbs 25:16:** Have you found honey? Eat *only* what you need, that you not have it in excess and vomit it.

Seek No Rich Food
This will reduce the temptation for recreational eating.

Sparing
> **Proverbs 25:27:** It is not good to eat much honey, nor is it glory to search out one's own glory.
> **28** Like a city that is broken into *and* without walls, is a man who has no control over his spirit.
> **Ecclesiastes 10:16:** Woe to you, O land, whose king is a lad and whose princes feast in the morning.
> **17** Blessed are you, O land, whose king is of nobility and whose princes eat at the appropriate time—for strength and not for drunkenness.

ADDITIONAL SCRIPTURE ON GLUTTONY:

Proverbs 30:21   Isaiah 22:12–14
Titus 2:12   Luke 21:33
1 Corinthians 5:11   1 Corinthians 6:13
Galatians 5:19–23

Exercise 2. Write a paragraph about gluttony and how it affects you. Include how you are going to minimize it. Keep your results to use in exercise 9.

CHAPTER TWO

PRIDE
(SUPERBIA)

PRIDE, n.

1. Inordinate self-esteem; an unreasonable conceit of one's own superiority in talents, beauty, wealth, accomplishments, rank or elevation in office, which manifests itself in lofty airs, distance, reserve, and often in contempt of others.

—Noah Webster's 1828 Dictionary of American English

H1343 An adjective meaning proud, haughty. The word describes an attitude of pride in persons that the Lord will judge at the right time. A whole nation can be depicted as haughty.

G2744 To boast, glory, exult, both in a good and bad sense.

SUMMARY

Pride is a close second to gluttony for being considered the worst of the seven sins. It frequently results in boasting and wrath. This was condemned by the ancient philosophers as a moral vice. Modern psychiatry classifies it as the mental illness of egomania. Pride takes many forms.

There are many Scriptures about pride. You probably can quote from memory at least part of the following famous story:

Luke 18:9: And He also told this parable to some people who trusted in themselves that they were righteous, and viewed others with contempt:
10 "Two men went up into the temple to pray, one a Pharisee and the other a tax collector.

11 "The Pharisee stood and was praying this to himself: 'God, I thank You that I am not like other people: swindlers, unjust, adulterers, or even like this tax collector.
12 'I fast twice a week; I pay tithes of all that I get.'
13 "But the tax collector, standing some distance away, was even unwilling to lift up his eyes to heaven, but was beating his breast, saying, 'God, be merciful to me, the sinner!'
14 "I tell you, this man went to his house justified rather than the other; for everyone who exalts himself will be humbled, but he who humbles himself will be exalted."

Here is another well-known passage:

Luke 14:11: For everyone who exalts himself will be humbled, and he who humbles himself will be exalted.

GENERAL CONDEMNATION

Proverbs 16:5: Everyone who is proud in heart is an abomination to the LORD; Assuredly, he will not be unpunished.

Pride can be communal. Back around 1990, several cities in Silicon Valley were planning to have playhouses for stage performances, complete with paid staffs. There were already stages available at schools and city centers that were rarely, if ever, used for plays. The playhouse was just a status symbol for the vulgarians—culturally lower-class people with wealth.

Being proud is different from having pride. You can be proud that your children have happy marriages. You can have pride of craftsmanship; you are happy that you did a good job and that others will benefit from it.

Pride can manifest itself in two basic ways: internal and external. The internal ways are observable only by God; the external ones by most everyone. Both types will damage your soul.

INTERNAL PRIDE

Arrogance

Proverbs 8:13: The fear of the LORD is to hate evil; Pride and arrogance and the evil way and the perverted mouth, I hate.

One form is considering God and society lucky that you exist. I once had a consulting job terminated because I did not stand up and cheer that my contact with the company was God's gift to the civilized world because he owned two old, dilapidated Cadillacs.

Another form is thinking that you are better than others because of some mass-produced consumer product you own or your ancestry, or bra size or wardrobe, or where you take your vacations, or some television program on DVD that you watch. The introductory level art appreciation lectures, *Civilization* by Clark, is one specific example of the latter. This program was intended for the mass-market British television audience back when the average adult had less than twelve years of schooling. Liking a program aimed at an eighth-grade intellectual level audience is no sign of advanced cultural achievement in an adult.

Pride can have disastrous effects on others. My late father let three fortunes pass by because he did not want to get expert legal advice about collecting them. Seeking outside advice would mean that he was not wise beyond the lot of mortals. He made the strangest excuses about why he let the fortunes pass.

Socrates pointed out in public that a government official was not talented. The official had enough political clout that he arranged for Socrates to be falsely charged with a crime and killed.

Pertinacity

One disastrous result of pride is refusing to admit a mistake. You continually repeat the mistake and repeatedly suffer the consequences. You may have heard the story from the 1939–1945 war where the incompetent military officer was trying to fit square pegs into round holes. His solution was to get a bigger hammer.

Back around 1940–1945 it was observed that some public officials were making decisions that put the U.S. at a disadvantage. It was proposed that these people were foreign agents. Journalists and academics rebutted these accusations. Then in 1990, the government declassified one of the code-breaking activities during the war. This one code, named *Venona*, was the breaking of Soviet communications with its agents in the U.S. About 450 government officials were identified as Soviet agents, including the top three advisors to President Roosevelt. Some other agents could not be identified. After this revelation, the journalists and academics came up with excuses why these people were not Soviet spies after all, and therefore their earlier evaluations were not mistaken.

Imprudence
You think that you can beat the odds. This is commonly combined with pertinacity. No matter how

many times the odds are not beaten, it is tried again with repeated losses.

One of my neighbors went through many cycles of leaving valuables in plain view and their being stolen.

Hubris

You know what is best for others even though they disagree. A severe form of this is wanting laws to force others to comply with what you specify. You have probably heard of the terms "educated fool" and "ivory tower theorists."

Elation

You are happy at the misfortunes of others. I once worked with a fellow who was always pointing out trivial mistakes to the people who made them. It did not take long for everyone to notice that he did not have the smarts to notice their less trivial mistakes.

EXTERNAL PRIDE

Disobedience

You know more than the experts and do not follow

their directions. My late father would ignore parts of equipment manuals when they conflicted with his hobby level technical knowledge. He did not notice that this caused the equipment to operate in a substandard way.

Boasting—Flattery

> **Jude 1:16:** These are murmurers, complainers, walking after their own lusts; and their mouth speaketh great swelling *words*, having men's persons in admiration because of advantage. (KJV)

This describes the actions of certain people disapproved of by God. Notice the "speak great swelling words" that today would be called boasting with their mouth. Boasting can also be done visually with flashy possessions. This reminds me of the saying, "Talkers seldom do and doers seldom talk."

I have seen several miserable marriages caused by the woman selecting the most prolific boaster for a husband. After it was too late, she learned that people boast the most about what they are most lacking. The last phrase in the Scripture passage forbids flattery or being a toady. I am afraid that many people try to flatter God by piling extra titles on Him or having red ink in their Bibles.

I have seen several engineers who spot imaginary problems and then became the self-proclaimed hero by "fixing" them.

> **Psalms 12:3:** May the LORD cut off all flattering lips, the tongue that speaks great things.
> **Proverbs 25:14:** *Like* clouds and wind without rain is a man who boasts of his gifts falsely.

One common form of boasting is collecting trophies or experiences and prominently displaying them. In the small, rural town where my parents lived, there was a sporting goods store. The owner started a trophy business in the back room. It quickly expanded and he sold the sporting goods store and operated the trophy shop from another, much larger premises. I suspect that many of these trophies were self-awarded.

Hypocrisy—False Front

This is pretending to be better or more talented than you are, verbally, in writing, or visually. I am reminded of the saying: You buy things you do not need with money you do not have in order to have mental illness delusions of impressing people who do not notice that you exist.

Overdressing is one example. In Silicon Valley, the more formally dressed someone is and the flashier car they drive, the more likely it is that they lack talent.

I know of a case of a British religious leader who wears an article of clothing, which is a badge of identification for past and present members of a famous, elite British military unit. This person has never served in the military.

Another example involves the manager of the literary estate of a deceased celebrity. This manager only gives permission to publishers if he can write the book introduction where he makes false claims about his relationship with the celebrity, his own education level, and imagined examples of the celebrity praising him.

Malice—Swelling of Heart
This is when you retain secret knowledge so that others fail. You can step in and be the big hero who rescues the situation.

Insolence
This is despising others who have lower opinions of you than you have of yourself.

> **Proverbs 13:10:** Through insolence comes nothing but strife, but wisdom is with those who receive counsel.

Contumely
This is expressing your "superiority" by using insulting language towards those who you despise. I know of a case where an employee of a service company insulted the customers. He was quickly fired.

Presumption
This is where you think that you are more talented than others are and take off like a bull in a china shop with disastrous results. Martin Luther calls this

"jumping in with your spurs on." Today it is called "knowing enough to be dangerous."

Back in the 1939–1945 war, the Germans used an electro-mechanical encryption machine, *Enigma*, for their most important messages. The receiving military units would then make quotation extracts and send them to their subordinate units in an easier to break code. By knowing the contents of the enigma-encrypted message, the code breakers at Bletchley Park were able to find the key for the day and decode all of the day's messages. Several British government officials tried hard to prevent the "wasted efforts" of cracking low-level codes when it was the enigma code that was important.

Irreverence

This is not giving respect to superiors or admiring those superior to you.

> **Acts 23:5:** And Paul said, "I was not aware, brethren, that he was high priest; for it is written, 'YOU SHALL NOT SPEAK EVIL OF A RULER OF YOUR PEOPLE.'"

Vainglory
This is a more severe case of hypocrisy where you honestly believe your false front.

> **Philippians 2:3:** *Let* nothing *be done* through strife or vainglory; but in lowliness of mind let each esteem other better than themselves.
> **4** Look not every man on his own things, but every man also on the things of others. (KJV)
> **Galatians 6:3:** For if anyone thinks he is something when he is nothing, he deceives himself.

I once knew an Irish woman who believed the tall tales she frequently told about herself. This brought home to me the meaning of the word *blarney*.

Conceit and Self-Exaltation
A further symptom of this Deadly Sin is frequently doing things to attract attention to yourself. I once received an advertisement to be included in a *Who's Who of Intellectuals* book. They provided a writing service for functionally illiterate people who could not write a few paragraphs describing their ideas for

the world to admire. I am reminded of the concept that genuinely talented people do not think about it and do not notice if anyone recognizes their talents. They just act like ordinary folks.

I know of several tragic cases where someone's showing off resulted in their death or permanent disability. Some people perform acts of violence in order to get the publicity from journalists' coverage. I wonder how much reduction in such crimes would result if the journalists ignored them.

Ambition

This is wanting to achieve something beyond what your talent would allow. You may remember the term "Victorian Folly."

A Warning

> **Psalms 40:4:** How blessed is the man who has made the LORD his trust, and has not turned to the proud, nor to those who lapse into falsehood.

We are told to not be fooled by proud people.

God's Direct Disapproval of Pride

Luke 11:43: "Woe to you Pharisees! For you love the chief seats in the synagogues and the respectful greetings in the market places.

44 "Woe to you! For you are like concealed tombs, and the people who walk over *them* are unaware *of it*."

Mark 7:21: "For from within, out of the heart of men, proceed the evil thoughts, fornications, thefts, murders, adulteries,

22 deeds of coveting *and* wickedness, *as well as* deceit, sensuality, envy, slander, pride *and* foolishness.

23 "All these evil things proceed from within and defile the man."

The Results of Pride

Proverbs 11:2: When pride comes, then comes dishonor, but with the humble is wisdom.

Proverbs 15:25: The LORD will tear down the house of the proud, but He will establish the boundary of the widow.

Isaiah 2:12: For the LORD of hosts will have a day of reckoning Against everyone who is proud and lofty And against everyone who is lifted up, That he may be abased.

Malachi 4:1: "For behold, the day is coming, burning like a furnace; and all the arrogant and every evildoer will be chaff; and the day that is coming will set them ablaze," says the LORD of hosts, "so that it will leave them neither root nor branch."

Cures for Pride

This is also an internal sin. Dorothy L. Sayers had observed that, because of our fallen natures, most people admire pride and avarice in others. First, you have to admit that you commit this sin. Whenever you are tempted to have a proud thought or boast, get in touch with your motives. You will probably have a good laugh at how stupid and trivial your motive was. Memorize some of the verses above and repeat them to yourself. Print some out on a card and have it on display at the location you frequently succumb to pride. Think of:

Luke 13:30: "And behold, *some* are last who will be first and *some* are first who will be last."

Psalms 37:11: But the meek shall inherit the earth; and shall delight themselves in the abundance of peace. (KJV)

Proverbs 29:23: A man's pride will bring him low, but a humble spirit will obtain honor.

In your daily prayers ask for help on this. Instead of thinking of people who are less talented than you are, think of the vast number of those who are more talented and by an astronomical margin.

Chaucer suggests practicing humility.

Humility of Heart
Do not despise others.
Admit your minor worth in God's sight.
Do not be concerned that others under-
evaluate you.

Do not feel bad when experiencing
    humiliation.

Humility of Mouth
    Have temperate speech.
    Have humble speech.
    Have a true evaluation of yourself.
    Praise others.

Humility of Actions
    Put the needs of others before yours.
    Choose the lowest place.
    Accept good advice.
    Follow others that have authority over you.

ADDITIONAL SCRIPTURE ON PRIDE:

Psalms 26:4

Psalms 73:3–20

Psalms 138:6

Proverbs 12:11

Proverbs 21:4

Proverbs 27:2

Psalms 36:11

Psalms 119:37

Proverbs 6:16–18

Proverbs 14:23

Proverbs 26:12

Proverbs 28:11

Proverbs 30:8–9

Ecclesiastes 4:8

Isaiah 23:9

Jeremiah 49:16

Daniel 4:37

Obadiah 1:3–4

2 Timothy 3:1–5

1 Peter 1:14–16

2 Peter 1:4

Ecclesiastes 2:10–11

Isaiah 5:21

Isaiah 25:11

Jeremiah 50:31–32

Daniel 5:20

1 Timothy 3:6

James 4:6

1 Peter 3:3–4

2 Peter 2:18

Exercise 3. Write a paragraph about pride and how it affects you. Include how you are going to minimize it. Keep your results for use in exercise 9.

CHAPTER THREE

LUST
(LUXURIA)

LUST, n.
1. Longing desire; eagerness to possess or enjoy; as the lust of gain.
2. Concupiscence; carnal appetite; unlawful desire of carnal pleasure.
3. Evil propensity; depraved affections and desires.

LUST, v.i.
1. To desire eagerly; to long; with after.
2. To have carnal desire; to desire eagerly the gratification of carnal appetite.

3. To have irregular or inordinate desires.
4. To list; to like.

—Noah Webster's 1828 Dictionary of American English

H2183 A masculine noun meaning fornication, prostitution, adultery, idolatry.

H5691 A feminine noun meaning lust. It refers to inordinate love, sensual desire, lust.

H8457 A noun meaning whoredom, prostitution.

G1939 Strong desire, longing, lust. Irregular and inordinate desire, appetite, lust. Generally to satisfy the carnal appetites; The lust of the flesh means carnal desires, appetites. Spoken of impure desire, lewdness. By metonymy, lust, i.e., an object of impure desire, that which is lusted after.

SUMMARY

Lust is a driving force to do things that are harmful to you, usually for some useless reason and with the consequences that you come out with a net harm from doing it. It includes much more than wanting to be sexual. The Old Testament used it as a metaphor for worshiping idols.

My father lusted after ease and took a cushy job that had low pay, and our family lived in economic straits because of it. One of my women friends took an otherwise unsuitable job because it allowed her to wear flashy clothes in public. Some people lust after an expensive lifestyle, spend all of their wealth on it, and do not save for their retirement. I heard of a widow who complained that her rent should not be raised because her late husband wore custom-made suits.

There was a news story some years back about a country club that secretly induced a celebrity to join so that people who lusted after the social prestige of associating with a celebrity would be willing to pay more for membership. The agreement with the celebrity included an exit clause where he would be paid a large fraction of the future membership price when he resigned his membership. This would have been kept private except for the country club refusing to buy back the celebrity's resigned membership and the case went public with a lawsuit filed by the celebrity.

SCRIPTURES ON LUST

We will list these under four headings.

Lust for Sex

Proverbs 6:25: Do not desire her beauty in your heart, nor let her capture you with her eyelids.

Matthew 5:28: But I say to you that everyone who looks at a woman with lust for her has already committed adultery with her in his heart.

Lust for Other Things

Psalms 78:18: And they tempted God in their heart by asking meat for their lust. (KJV)

Matthew Henry says:

[They were disrespectful to God] by desiring, or rather demanding, that which he had not thought fit to give them: *They asked meat for their lust.* God had given them meat for their hunger. But this would not serve; they must have meat for their lust, dainties and varieties to gratify a luxurious appetite.

Romans 7:7: What shall we say then? *Is* the law sin? God forbid. Nay, I had not known sin, but by the law: for I had not known lust, except the law had said, Thou shalt not covet. (KJV)

Matthew Henry says:

By lust he means sin dwelling in us, sin in its first motions and workings, the corrupt principle. This he came to know when the law said, *Thou shalt not covet.* The law spoke in other language than the scribes and Pharisees made it to speak in; it spoke in the spiritual sense and meaning of it. By this he knew that lust was sin and a very sinful sin, that those motions and desires of the heart towards sin which never came into act were sinful, exceedingly sinful.

1 Corinthians 10:6: Now these things were our examples, to the intent we should not lust after evil things, as they also lusted. (KJV)

Adultery—Prostitution
Leviticus 20:10: If *there is* a man who commits adultery with another man's wife, one who commits adultery with his friend's wife, the adulterer and the adulteress shall surely be put to death.

This execution was to be done by the judicial system, and not by individuals. Notice that it is the act and not the temptation that is the grounds for execution.

Proverbs 5:3: For the lips of an adulteress drip honey And smoother than oil is her speech;
4 But in the end she is bitter as wormwood, Sharp as a two-edged sword.

5 Her feet go down to death, Her steps take hold of Sheol.

1 Corinthians 6:15: Do you not know that your bodies are members of Christ? Shall I then take away the members of Christ and make them members of a prostitute? May it never be!

Ephesians 5:5: For this ye know, that no whoremonger, nor unclean person, nor covetous man, who is an idolater, hath any inheritance in the kingdom of Christ and of God. (KJV)

Homosexuality

I know that this is very unpopular these days, but God owns heaven and sets the rules on whom He lets in and states the rules in the Bible. This is very much like the immigration laws in a certain country. One of many requirements for being allowed entry is having a net worth of over half a million dollars. No amount of wishful thinking, or sermons to the contrary, will let you in without the wealth.

Leviticus 18:22: You shall not lie with a male as one lies with a female; it is an abomination.

Leviticus 20:13: If *there is* a man who lies with a male as those who lie with a woman, both of them have committed a detestable act; they shall surely be put to death. Their blood guiltiness is upon them.

This execution was to be done by the judicial system, and not by individuals. As in adultery, it is the act and not the temptation that is the grounds for execution.

The Results of Lust

1 Timothy 6:9: But they that will be rich fall into temptation and a snare, and *into* many foolish and hurtful lusts, which drown men in destruction and perdition. (KJV)

James 1:14: But each one is tempted when he is carried away and enticed by his own lust.

15 Then when lust has conceived, it gives

birth to sin; and when sin is accomplished, it brings forth death. (KJV)

James 4:1: What is the source of quarrels and conflicts among you? Is not the source your pleasures that wage war in your members?

2 You lust and do not have; *so* you commit murder. You are envious and cannot obtain; *so* you fight and quarrel. You do not have because you do not ask.

3 You ask and do not receive, because you ask with wrong motives, so that you may spend *it* on your pleasures.

4 You adulteresses, do you not know that friendship with the world is hostility toward God? Therefore whoever wishes to be a friend of the world makes himself an enemy of God. (KJV)

Cures for Lust

As in all of the sins, you have to admit that you do it before you can do something about it. Get in touch with your motives. Avoid situations that produce lust. Pray when you have undesirable thoughts. Become

busy doing something useful. Memorize some of
the Scriptures above and say them to yourself. Print
some on a card, then put in locations where you are
most tempted.

Chaucer suggests practicing the following virtues: chastity, continence, and seeking scriptural
help to overcome lust.

Chastity

Galatians 5:16: *This* I say then, Walk in the
Spirit, and ye shall not fulfill the lust of the
flesh. (KJV)
2 Timothy 2:22: Now flee from youthful
lusts and pursue righteousness, faith, love
and peace, with those who call on the Lord
from a pure heart.

Continence

Galatians 5:24: And they that are Christ's
have crucified the flesh with the affections
and lusts. (KJV)
Titus 2:12: Teaching us that, denying
ungodliness and worldly lusts, we should live

soberly, righteously, and godly, in this present world. (KJV)

SCRIPTURAL HELP OVERCOMING LUST

Romans 13:14: But put on the Lord Jesus Christ, and make no provision for the flesh in regard to *its* lusts.

Galatians 5:24: And they that are Christ's have crucified the flesh with the affections and lusts. (KJV)

1 Peter 2:11: Beloved, I urge you as aliens and strangers to abstain from fleshly lusts which wage war against the soul.

1 John 2:17: The world is passing away, and *also* its lusts; but the one who does the will of God lives forever.

ADDITIONAL SCRIPTURE ON LUST:

Genesis 3:5–6

Proverbs 30:20

Romans 1:24–27

Psalms 81:12

Mark 4:19

Romans 6:12–13

1 Thessalonians 4:5
Ephesians 2:3
1 Corinthians 6:9–11
James 4:5
2 Timothy 4:3
1 Peter 4:1–3
2 Peter 3:3
Jude 1:16–18

Galatians 5:19–21
Ephesians 4:22–24
Titus 3:3
2 Timothy 3:6–7
1 Peter 4:32
2 Peter 2:18
1 John 2:15–17

Exercise 4. Write a paragraph about lust and how it affects you. Include measures you will take to minimize it. Keep your results for use in exercise 9.

CHAPTER FOUR

WRATH
(IRA)

AN'GER, n. ang'ger. [L. ango, to choke strangle, vex; whence angor, vexation, anguish, the quinsy, angina. Gr. to strangle, to strain or draw together to vex. The primary sense is to press, squeeze, make narrow; Heb. to strangle.]

1. A violent passion of the mind excited by a real or supposed injury; usually accompanied with a propensity to take vengeance, or to obtain satisfaction from the offending party. This passion, however, varies in degrees of violence, and in ingenuous minds may be attended only with a desire to reprove or chide the offender.

Anger is also excited by an injury offered to a relation, friend or party to which one is attached; and some degrees of it may be excited by cruelty, injustice or oppression offered to those with whom one has no immediate connection, or even to the community of which one is a member. Nor is it unusual to see something of this passion roused by gross absurdities in others, especially in controversy or discussion. Anger may be inflamed until it rises to rage and a temporary delirium.

—Noah Webster's 1828 Dictionary of American English

H2534 A noun meaning wrath, heat. Figuratively, it can signify anger, hot displeasure, indignation, poison, or rage.

H5678 A feminine noun meaning wrath, fury. It implies an overflowing anger. When the word is used of people, it usually describes a fault of character, a cruel anger; associated with pride.

H6225 A verb meaning to smoke, to be angry, to be furious. The literal meaning of this Hebrew word is to smolder or smoke. Metaphorically, it was used by the psalmist to convey the idea of fuming anger.

G2372 To move impetuously, particularly as the air or wind, a violent motion or passion of the mind. Anger, wrath, indignation.

G3710 Wrath. To make angry, provoke.

SUMMARY

Wrath is frequently irrational anger. It is associated with revenge and indignation. There is sudden wrath and long-term wrath. Long-term wrath causes body stress and degrades your health. One sudden form is when your efforts to do something, which is motivated by one of the other deadly sins, is frustrated. What makes this form of anger so tragic is that it is frequently the case that God has intervened and tried to keep you from committing these sins or doing something stupid. Another cause is your false fronts being noticed as such by others. An old saying goes, "Decide in haste, regret at leisure." Passion takes away our wit and reason. It sometimes motivates us to harm others.

Proverbs 14:17: A quick-tempered man acts foolishly, And a man of evil devices is hated.
Proverbs 14:29: He who is slow to anger has great understanding, but he who is quick-tempered exalts folly.

If you are attuned to God, He will frequently keep you from doing stupid things. One personal example of this help occurred to me about thirty years ago. I was intent on getting a job at a company in a small town. God blocked it. He then had a person recommend me to a high-technology company in a large industrial area where I received a wide variety of experiences that further improved my technical skills. While I was employed there, several managers remarked that I could do much better as a consultant. I tried the consulting route and have had more fun and slightly higher income from doing it. It has also given me the free time to write books that I hope have improved the righteousness level of others and inspired them to have a closer walk with the Lord.

One amusing example of wrath involved Jonah (of whale fame) after Nineveh repented:

Jonah 4:5: Then Jonah went out from the city and sat east of it. There he made a shelter for himself and sat under it in the shade until he could see what would happen in the city.

6 So the LORD God appointed a plant and it grew up over Jonah to be a shade over his head to deliver him from his discomfort. And Jonah was extremely happy about the plant.

7 But God appointed a worm when dawn came the next day and it attacked the plant and it withered.

8 When the sun came up God appointed a scorching east wind, and the sun beat down on Jonah's head so that he became faint and begged with all his soul to die, saying, "Death is better to me than life."

9 Then God said to Jonah, "Do you have good reason to be angry about the plant?"

And he said, "I have good reason to be angry, even to death."

He is angry that God did not give him more shade and makes a churlish reply to God. God's gentle reply is an example of how longsuffering He is toward our weaknesses.

Another well-known passage involves a talking donkey:

Numbers 22:26: The angel of the LORD went further, and stood in a narrow place where there was no way to turn to the right hand or the left.

27 When the donkey saw the angel of the LORD, she lay down under Balaam; so Balaam was angry and struck the donkey with his stick.

28 And the LORD opened the mouth of the donkey, and she said to Balaam, "What have I done to you, that you have struck me these three times?"

29 Then Balaam said to the donkey, "Because

you have made a mockery of me! If there had been a sword in my hand, I would have killed you by now."

30 The donkey said to Balaam, "Am I not your donkey on which you have ridden all your life to this day? Have I ever been accustomed to do so to you?" And he said, "No."

31 Then the LORD opened the eyes of Balaam, and he saw the angel of the LORD standing in the way with his drawn sword in his hand; and he bowed all the way to the ground.

32 The angel of the LORD said to him, "Why have you struck your donkey these three times? Behold, I have come out as an adversary, because your way was contrary to me.

33 "But the donkey saw me and turned aside from me these three times. If she had not turned aside from me, I would surely have killed you just now, and let her live."

This is one of my favorite passages. Balaam is so angry that he does not notice he is holding an intelligent conversation with a dumb animal. The poor donkey has saved Balaam's life. As stated earlier, wrath takes away our wit and reason.

MORE SCRIPTURE ON WRATH

Scripture has a lot to say about wrath.

Some Wrath is Appropriate
In some circumstances there is "righteous" wrath that is motivated by observing others disobeying God. This is acceptable. One example is when Moses saw the idolatry of his flock.

> **Exodus 32:19:** It came about, as soon as Moses came near the camp, that he saw the calf and the dancing; and Moses' anger burned, and he threw the tablets from his hands and shattered them at the foot of the mountain.

Another example is from being influenced by God.

Judges 14:19: Then the Spirit of the LORD came upon him [Samson] mightily, and he went down to Ashkelon and killed thirty of them and took their spoil and gave the changes *of clothes* to those who told the riddle. And his anger burned, and he went up to his father's house.

God Disapproves of Wrath

James 1:19: *This* you know, my beloved brethren. But everyone must be quick to hear, slow to speak *and* slow to anger;
20 for the anger of man does not achieve the righteousness of God.

Matthew Henry says:

[This is] to restrain the workings of passion. This lesson we should learn under afflictions; and this we shall learn if we are indeed begotten again by the word of truth. For thus the connection stands—An angry and hasty spirit is soon provoked to ill things by afflictions, and errors and ill opinions become prevalent through the workings of our own vile and vain affections; but the renewing grace of God and the word of the gospel teach us to subdue these: *Wherefore, my beloved brethren, let every man be swift to hear, slow to speak, slow to wrath*, James 1:19. *Wrath* is a human thing, and the wrath of man stands opposed to the righteousness of God.

Effects of Wrath

Proverbs 19:19: *A man* of great anger will bear the penalty, for if you rescue *him*, you will only have to do it again.

Matthew Henry says:

As we read this, it intimates, in short, that angry men never want [lack] woe. Those that are of strong, or rather headstrong, passions, commonly bring themselves and their families into trouble by vexatious suits and quarrels and the provocations they give; they are still smarting, in one instance or other, for their ungoverned heats; and, if their friends deliver them out of one trouble, they will quickly involve themselves in another, and they *must do it again*, all which troubles to themselves and others would be prevented if they would mortify their passions and get the rule of their own spirits.

Ecclesiastes 7:8: The end of a matter is better than its beginning; Patience of spirit is better than haughtiness of spirit.
9 Do not be eager in your heart to be angry, for anger resides in the bosom of fools.
Job 5:2: For anger slays the foolish man, and jealousy kills the simple.
Proverbs 29:22: An angry man stirs up strife, and a hot-tempered man abounds in transgression.

I once knew a woman who was enamored with a violent man and intended to marry him. She did not think ahead and ponder the probability that he would be violent to her. He would also have the problem of keeping a job.

Cure For Wrath

As in all of the sins, you have to admit that you do it before you can do something about it. Get in touch with your motives. Wrath is frequently triggered when your efforts to commit pride, avarice, or lust are thwarted. Avoid situations that produce wrath. Examine the cause of your wrath. You will be surprised and amused at what stupid and trivial situations have caused it. Pray when you start to have wrath. Concentrate on useful goals in your life. Memorize some of the Scriptures above and say them to yourself. Print some on a card, then put in locations where you are most tempted. Repeat to yourself, "Decide in haste, regret at leisure." Recognize that God is saving you from some disaster.

Chaucer suggests practicing the following virtues: meekness, patience, and love.

Meekness

1 Peter 3:4: But *let it be* the hidden person of the heart, with the imperishable quality of a gentle and quiet spirit, which is precious in the sight of God.

Proverbs 15:18: A hot-tempered man stirs up strife, but the slow to anger calms a dispute.

Patience

James 3:17: But the wisdom from above is first pure, then peaceable, gentle, reasonable, full of mercy and good fruits, unwavering, without hypocrisy.

Proverbs 16:32: He who is slow to anger is better than the mighty, and he who rules his spirit, than he who captures a city.

Love

Matthew 5:43: You have heard that it was said, "YOU SHALL LOVE YOUR NEIGHBOR and hate your enemy."

44 But I say to you, love your enemies and pray for those who persecute you.

Galatians 5:19: Now the deeds of the flesh are evident, which are: immorality, impurity, sensuality,

20 idolatry, sorcery, enmities, strife, jealousy, outbursts of anger, disputes, dissensions, factions,

21 envying, drunkenness, carousing, and things like these, of which I forewarn you, just as I have forewarned you, that those who practice such things will not inherit the kingdom of God.

22 But the fruit of the Spirit is love, joy, peace, patience, kindness, goodness, faithfulness,

23 gentleness, self-control; against such things there is no law.

Notice verse 21, which says that committing these sins is a sign that you will not enter heaven. In other words, these are a symptom of a spiritual disease, and not the cause of it.

ADDITIONAL SCRIPTURE ON WRATH:

Psalms 37:8 –9	Psalms 101:5
Proverbs 6:34	Proverbs 12:16
Proverbs 21:19	Proverbs 21:23
Proverbs 22:24	Proverbs 25:28
Proverbs 30:33	Matthew 5:22
Romans 12:19–21	Ephesians 4:31
Colossians 3:8	1 Timothy 2:8
1 John 2:9	1 John 3:15
1 John 4:20–21	1 Corinthians 13:4–8

Exercise 5. Write a paragraph about wrath and how it affects you. Include measures you will take to minimize it. Keep your results for use in exercise 9.

CHAPTER FIVE

AVARICE
(AVARITIA)

AV'ARICE, n. [L. avaritia, from avarus, from aveo, to covet.]

An inordinate desire of gaining and possessing wealth; covetousness; greediness or insatiable desire of gain.

Avarice sheds a blasting influence over the finest affections and sweetest comforts of mankind.

—Noah Webster's 1828 Dictionary of American English

H2530 A verb meaning to take pleasure in, to desire, to lust, to covet, to be desirable, to desire passionately. The verb can mean to desire intensely even in its simple stem: the tenth commandment prohibits desiring to the point of coveting, such as a neighbor's house, wife, or other assets. Israel was not to covet silver or gold, or the fields and lands of others.

G4123 To be covetous. One who wants more, a person covetous of something that others have, a defrauder for gain.

SUMMARY

Other words for this are greed and covet. This sin is partially overlapping with gluttony and lust. There are three types of avarice beyond amassing wealth. One type is wanting a one-of-a-kind thing that belongs to someone else, such as their spouse. Another is wanting a mass-produced item. Much of advertising is based on exploiting this sin. I have known some women who would throw out attractive clothes that were in good condition in order to make room for new purchases. Both C. S. Lewis and Dorothy L. Sayers have condemned advertising for inducing people to spend their money foolishly. The third is hoarding so that you do not give to charity. You can probably quote the following passages from memory:

Matthew 6:24: No one can serve two masters; for either he will hate the one and love the other, or he will be devoted to one and despise the other. You cannot serve God and wealth.

Exodus 20:17: You shall not covet your neighbor's house; you shall not covet your neighbor's wife or his male servant or his female servant or his ox or his donkey or anything that belongs to your neighbor.

Mark 10:23: And Jesus, looking around, and said to His disciples, "How hard it will be for those who are wealthy to enter the kingdom of God!"

24 The disciples were amazed at His words. But Jesus answered again and said to them, "Children, how hard it is to enter the kingdom of God!

25 "It is easier for a camel to go through the

eye of a needle than for a rich man to enter the kingdom of God."

Matthew 6:19: Do not store up for yourselves treasures on earth, where moth and rust destroy, and where thieves break in and steal.

20 But store up for yourselves treasures in heaven, where neither moth nor rust destroys, and where thieves do not break in or steal;

21 for where your treasure is, there your heart will be also.

In effect, you become possessed by your possessions. Possessions become idols.

Colossians 3:5: Therefore consider the members of your earthly body as dead to immorality, impurity, passion, evil desire, and greed, which amounts to idolatry.

6 For it is because of these things that the wrath of God will come upon the sons of disobedience.

Matthew Henry has the following to say about avarice:

Worldly-mindedness is as common and as fatal a symptom of hypocrisy as any other, for by no sin can Satan have a surer and faster hold of the soul, under the cloak of a visible and passable profession of religion, than by this; and therefore Christ, having warned us against coveting *the praise of men*, proceeds next to warn us against coveting the wealth of the world; in this also we must take heed, lest we be as the hypocrites are, and do as they do: the fundamental error that they are guilty of is, that they choose the world for *their reward*; we must therefore take heed of hypocrisy and worldly-mindedness, in the choice we make of our treasure, our end, and our masters.

A *good caution* against making *the things that are seen*, that *are temporal*, our best things, and placing our happiness in them. *Lay not up for yourselves treasures upon earth*. We must not covet an abundance of these things, nor be still grasping at more and more of them, and adding to them, as men do to that which is their treasure, as never knowing when we have enough. We must not confide in them for futurity, to be our security and supply in time to come; we must not say to the gold, *Thou art my hope*. We must not content ourselves with them, as all we need or desire: we must be content with a little for our passage, but not with all for our portion.

There are *treasures in heaven*, as sure as there are on this earth; and those in heaven are the only true *treasure*. It is our wisdom to *lay up* our *treasure in* those *treasures*; to give all diligence to make sure our title to eternal life through Jesus Christ, and to depend upon that as our happiness, and look upon all things here below with a holy contempt, as not worthy to be compared with it. *Where your treasure is*, on earth or in heaven, *there will your heart be*. We must take heed of hypocrisy and worldly-mindedness in choosing the *end we look at*. We must take heed of hypocrisy and worldly-mindedness in choosing the master we serve. Matthew 6:24: *No man can serve two masters.* Serving *two masters* is contrary to *the single eye;* for *the eye* will be to the master's hand, Psalms 123:1, Psalms 123:2. The application of it to the business in hand. *Ye cannot serve God and Mammon. Mammon* is a Syriac word, that signifies gain; so that whatever in this world is, or is accounted by us to be, *gain* (Philemon 3:7), is *mammon. Whatever is in the world, the lust of the flesh, the lust of the eye, and the pride of life*, is *mammon.* To some their belly is their *mammon*, and they serve that (Philemon 3:19); to others their ease, their sleep, their sports and pastimes, are their *mammon* (Proverbs 6:9); to others worldly riches (James 4:13); to others honours and preferments; the praise and applause of men was the Pharisees' *mammon;* in a word, self, the unity in which the world's trinity centres, sensual, secular self, is the *mammon* which cannot be served in conjunction with *God;* for if it be served, it is in competition with him and in contradiction to him.

General Condemnation

Micah 2:1: Woe to those who scheme iniquity, who work out evil on their beds! When morning comes, they do it, for it is in the power of their hands.
2 They covet fields and then seize *them*, and houses, and take *them* away. They rob a man and his house, a man and his inheritance.
Isaiah 5:8: Woe to those who add house to house *and* join field to field, until there is no more room, so that you have to live alone in the midst of the land!

I am reliably informed that in the State of Nevada there are some people who think that unless you own at least a square mile of useless desert, you are a nobody.

CURES FOR AVARICE

As in all of the sins, you have to admit that you do it before you can do something about it. Get in touch with your motives. Avarice is frequently triggered by advertising. Sometimes it is by pride. You may want some object as a status symbol. Avoid situations that produce avarice. Pray when you start to have avarice. Enjoy using the items you already own. Memorize some of the Scriptures above and say them to yourself. Print some on a card, then put in locations where you are most tempted.

1 Timothy 6:6: But godliness *actually* is a means of great gain when accompanied by contentment.
7 For we have brought nothing into the world, so we cannot take anything out of it either.
8 If we have food and covering, with these we shall be content.
9 But those who want to get rich fall into

temptation and a snare and many foolish
and harmful desires which plunge men into
ruin and destruction.

10 For the love of money is a root of all sorts
of evil, and some by longing for it have wan-
dered away from the faith and pierced themselves with many griefs.

Luke 12:15: Then He said to them, "Beware,
and be on your guard against every form of
greed; for not *even* when one has an abundance
does his life consist of his possessions."

Chaucer suggests practicing the following virtues: mercy, pity and charity, and generosity.

Mercy

Luke 10:33: But a [the famous good] Samaritan, who was on a journey, came upon him;
and when he saw him, he felt compassion,

34 and came to him and bandaged up his
wounds, pouring oil and wine on *them*; and
he put him on his own beast, and brought
him to an inn and took care of him.

Proverbs 14:21: He who despises his neighbor sins, but happy is he who is gracious to the poor.

Pity and Charity
Proverbs 21:26: All day long he is craving, while the righteous gives and does not hold back.

Generosity
Proverbs 22:9: He who is generous will be blessed, For he gives some of his food to the poor.

Luke 6:38: Give, and it will be given to you. They will pour into your lap a good measure—pressed down, shaken together, *and* running over. For by your standard of measure it will be measured to you in return.

Acts 20:35: In everything I showed you that by working hard in this manner you must help the weak and remember the words of the Lord Jesus, that He Himself said, "It is more blessed to give than to receive."

ADDITIONAL SCRIPTURE ON AVARICE:

Exodus 20:3–5

Proverbs 29:7

Ecclesiastes 4:6

Amos 8:4–7

Luke 12:16–21

Romans 13:9–10

Corinthians 6:9–10

1 Timothy 3:2–5

1 Kings 21:1–7

Proverbs 28:16

Ezekiel 16:49

Mark 7:21–23

John 12:3–6

1 Corinthians 5:1 1

Ephesians 5:3–5

Hebrews 13:5

ADDITIONAL SCRIPTURE ON GENEROSITY:

Psalms 41:1

Proverbs 11:24

Proverbs 28:27

1 John 3:17

Psalms 112:9

Proverbs 19:17

2 Corinthians 9:7

Exercise 6. Write a paragraph about avarice and how it affects you. Include measures you will take to minimize it. Keep your results for use in exercise 9.

CHAPTER SIX

ENVY
(INVIDIA)

EN'VY, v.t. [L. invideo, in and video, to see against, that is, to look with enmity.]

1. To feel uneasiness, mortification or discontent, at the sight of superior excellence, reputation or happiness enjoyed by another; to repine at another's prosperity; to fret or grieve one's self at the real or supposed superiority of another, and to hate him on that account.

2. To grudge; to withhold maliciously.

EN'VY, n. Pain, uneasiness, mortification or discontent excited by the sight of another's superiority or success, accompanied with some degree of hatred or malignity, and often or usually with a desire or an effort to depreciate the person, and with pleasure in seeing him depressed. Envy springs from pride, ambition or love, mortified that another has obtained what one has a strong desire to possess.

1. Rivalry; competition. [Little used.]

2. Malice; malignity.

3. Public odium; ill repute; invidiousness.

—Noah Webster's 1828 Dictionary of American English

H7520 A verb meaning to look with envy. It indicates looking at persons, keeping a hostile or envious eye on them.

G5355 Envy, jealousy, pain felt and malignity conceived at the sight of excellence or happiness.

SUMMARY

Envy is the inverse of avarice. Instead of wanting more for yourself, you want others to have less. Jealousy is closely allied to envy. Passive envy involves rejoicing in the misfortunes of others. Active envy is doing things to harm others. One example of the latter is wanting rich people to pay higher tax rates. Envy can be about noneconomic things. I have been told that when the Jaguar XKE came out, the British Labour government lowered the speed limit. Unscrupulous journalists frequently stimulate envy in voters in order to influence elections and legislation.

Two famous passages about envy are:

Proverbs 14:30: A sound heart *is* the life of the flesh, but envy the rottenness of the bones. (KJV)

Song of Solomon 8:6: Set me as a seal upon thine heart, as a seal upon thine arm; for love *is* strong as death; jealousy *is* cruel as the grave; the coals thereof *are* coals of fire, *which hath a* most vehement flame. (KJV)

SPECIFIC EXAMPLES OF ENVY

Sorrow for the Prosperity and Blessings of Others
You probably have heard of "house envy." There have been extreme cases of this in Silicon Valley

when someone in a run-down neighborhood wanted to tear down their house and build a better one. The neighbors went before the planning commission and wanted planning permission to be denied because it would "ruin the character of the neighborhood."

> **Psalms 49:16:** Do not be afraid when a man becomes rich, when the glory of his house is increased;
> **17** For when he dies he will carry nothing away; His glory will not descend after him.
> **Job 1:21:** And said, Naked came I out of my mother's womb, and naked shall I return thither the LORD gave, and the LORD hath taken away; blessed be the name of the LORD. (KJV)

Joy in the Harm of Others
Some time ago, a famous author of Christian books was very elderly and contracted a disease, which eventually killed him. Many people claimed that his death was God's condemnation of his books.

Malice

1 Peter 2:1: Therefore, putting aside all malice and all deceit and hypocrisy and envy and all slander.

Knowingly Attacks Truth

This causes some to not believe the truth and thus not benefit from the truth.

Acts 13:44: The next Sabbath nearly the whole city assembled to hear the word of the Lord.

45 But when the Jews saw the crowds, they were filled with jealousy and *began* contradicting the things spoken by Paul, and were blaspheming.

James 3:13: Who among you is wise and understanding? Let him show by his good behavior his deeds in the gentleness of wisdom.

14 But if you have bitter jealousy and selfish ambition in your heart, do not be arrogant and *so* lie against the truth.

15 This wisdom is not that which comes down from above, but is earthly, natural, demonic.

16 For where jealousy and selfish ambition exist, there is disorder and every evil thing.

17 But the wisdom from above is first pure, then peaceable, gentle, reasonable, full of mercy and good fruits, unwavering, without hypocrisy.

18 And the seed whose fruit is righteousness is sown in peace by those who make peace.

Attacks the Grace of God Given to Neighbors
This is so they will not take advantage of this grace.

Acts 13:8: But Elymas the magician (for so his name is translated) was opposing them [Paul on a missionary journey], seeking to turn the proconsul away from the faith.

Satan's plan backfired. There was a happy ending:

Acts 13:12: Then the proconsul believed when he saw what had happened, being amazed at the teaching of the Lord.

Disparagement of People Others Praise
Some groups think pastors who are self trained are better than those who are seminary trained. This is encouraged by the self-trained pastors.

Acts 23:5: And Paul said, "I was not aware, brethren, that he was high priest; for it is written, 'YOU SHALL NOT SPEAK EVIL OF A RULER OF YOUR PEOPLE.'"

Murmuring and Complaining
James 5:9: Do not complain, brethren, against one another, so that you yourselves may not be judged; behold, the Judge is standing right at the door.

Scorn
Proverbs 19:29: Judgments are prepared for scorners, and stripes for the back of fools.

Annoy Neighbors
Such as using the lawn mower early in the morning
or flaunting your possessions.

Accusations of Neighbors
I am reminded of the medical profession, which uses
two brass snakes on a pole as a symbol of their profession. This is from the Exodus where God told Moses
to make a bronze serpent to stop a plague of snakes:

> **Numbers 21:8:** Then the LORD said to
> Moses, "Make a fiery *serpent*, and set it on
> a standard; and it shall come about, that
> everyone who is bitten, when he looks at it,
> he will live."
> **9** And Moses made a bronze serpent and set
> it on the standard; and it came about, that if
> a serpent bit any man, when he looked to the
> bronze serpent, he lived.

Unfortunately, the bronze serpent later became
an idol-relic that was worshipped and had to be
destroyed:

2 Kings 18:4: He [King Hezekiah] removed the high places and broke down the *sacred* pillars and cut down the Asherah. He also broke in pieces the bronze serpent that Moses had made, for until those days the sons of Israel burned incense to it and it was called Nehushtan.

Some time ago, a splinter group claimed that, because of the use of this symbol, the members of the medical profession were secret snake worshippers of some ancient cult. As an old saying goes, "You can fool some of the people all of the time."

Regret the Blessings of Neighbors and Injure Them
One of my friends who had been successful in business retired to a small town in the Dakotas. After a few years, he noticed that whenever someone wanted to better themselves, others took active measures to keep the efforts from being successful.

Vandalism is another common form.

Ecclesiastes 4:4: Again, I considered all travail, and every right work, that for this a man is envied of his neighbour. This *is* also vanity and vexation of spirit. (KJV)

Fallen human nature never changes.

Romans 13:10: Love does no wrong to a neighbor; therefore love is *the* fulfillment of the law.

Hurt Neighbors Secretly
One example is not giving warnings of impending disasters. Another is not moving their property out of harm's way when they are absent. Giving false advice is yet another.

Spreading Rumors, Gossip About Others, and Slander
This includes listening to, repeating, and inventing stories.

Romans 1:28: And just as they did not see fit to acknowledge God any longer, God gave them over to a depraved mind, to do those things which are not proper,

29 being filled with all unrighteousness, wickedness, greed, evil; full of envy, murder, strife, deceit, malice; *they are* gossips,

30 slanderers, haters of God, insolent, arrogant, boastful, inventors of evil, disobedient to parents,

31 without understanding, untrustworthy, unloving, unmerciful;

32 and although they know the ordinance of God, that those who practice such things are worthy of death, they not only do the same, but also give hearty approval to those who practice them.

Exodus 20:16: You shall not bear false witness against your neighbor.

Proverbs 10:18: He who conceals hatred *has* lying lips, and he who spreads slander is a fool.

Proverbs 26:20: Where no wood is, *there* the fire goeth out: so where *there is* no talebearer, the strife ceaseth. (KJV)

Matthew 15:18: "But the things that proceed out of the mouth come from the heart, and those defile the man.
19 For out of the heart come evil thoughts, murders, adulteries, fornications, thefts, false witness, slanders.

Matthew Henry has some harsh words about this:

But that which comes out of the mouth, this defiles a man. We are polluted, not by the meat we eat with unwashen hands, but by the words we speak from an unsanctified heart; thus it is that *the mouth causeth the flesh to sin* (Ecclesiastes 5:6). Christ, in a former discourse, had laid a great stress upon our *words* (Matthew 12:36; Matthew 12:37); and that was intended for reproof and warning to those that caviled at him; this here is intended for reproof and warning to those that caviled at the disciples, and censured them. It is not the disciples that defile themselves with what they eat, but the Pharisees that defile themselves with what they speak spitefully and censoriously of them. Note, those who charge guilt upon others for transgressing the commandments of men, many times bring greater guilt upon themselves, by transgressing the law of God against rash judging. Those most defile themselves, who are most forward to censure the defilements of others.

Strife
This is causing discord so that people waste their energy on nonproductive and harmful activities.

Romans 13:13: Let us behave properly as in the day, not in carousing and drunkenness, not in sexual promiscuity and sensuality, not in strife and jealousy.

14 But put on the Lord Jesus Christ, and make no provision for the flesh in regard to *its* lusts.

1 Corinthians 3:3: For you are still fleshly.

For since there is jealousy and strife among you, are you not fleshly, and are you not walking like mere men?

Although not related to envy, the British were able to maintain their empire by causing strife between the subjects in each of their colonies. This way the subjects were left with little energy to fight the British. This was a form of "divide and conquer." Much of the harm in the third world today is caused by the colonial powers drawing national boundaries so that tribal groups are split between countries and warring groups are combined in one country.

One Historical Examples of Envy

Mark 15:9: Pilate answered them, saying, "Do you want me to release for you the King of the Jews?"

10 For he was aware that the chief priests had handed Him over because of envy.

11 But the chief priests stirred up the crowd *to ask* him to release Barabbas for them instead.

Cures for Envy

As in all of the sins, you have to admit that you do it before you can do something about it. Get in touch with your motives. Pray when you start to feel envy. Enjoy using the items you already own. Memorize some of the Scriptures above and say them to yourself. Print some on a card, then put in locations where you are most tempted.

Chaucer suggests practicing the following virtues: love neighbor as self, do charity and good do neighbor, love neighbors in your heart, and pray for and love your enemy.

Love neighbor as self

1 Corinthians 13:4: Love is patient, love is kind *and* is not jealous; love does not brag *and* is not arrogant,

5 does not act unbecomingly; it does not seek its own, is not provoked, does not take into account a wrong *suffered*,

6 does not rejoice in unrighteousness, but rejoices with the truth;

7 bears all things, believes all things, hopes all things, endures all things.

Do charity and good to neighbor
Luke 10:33: But a [the famous good] Samaritan, who was on a journey, came upon him; and when he saw him, he felt compassion,
34 and came to him and bandaged up his wounds, pouring oil and wine on *them*; and he put him on his own beast, and brought him to an inn and took care of him.

Love neighbors in your heart
Matthew 22:39: The second is like it, "YOU SHALL LOVE YOUR NEIGHBOR AS YOURSELF."

Pray for and love your enemy
Matthew 5:43: You have heard that it was said, "YOU SHALL LOVE YOUR NEIGHBOR and hate your enemy."
44 But I say to you, love your enemies and pray for those who persecute you.

ADDITIONAL SCRIPTURE ON ENVY:

Exodus 22:28
Proverbs 6:34
Romans 1:28–32
1 Corinthians 3:3
2 Corinthians 12:20
Peter 2:9–10

Job 5:2
Ecclesiastes 4:4
Galatians 5:19–26
1 Corinthians 13:4
1 Timothy 6:4–82

Exercise 7. Write a paragraph about envy and how it affects you. Include measures you will take to minimize it. Keep your results for use in exercise 9.

CHAPTER SEVEN

SLOTH
(ACEDIA)

SLOTH, n.

1. Slowness; tardiness

2. Disinclination to action or labor; sluggishness; laziness; idleness. They change their course to pleasure, ease and sloth. Sloth, like rust, consumes faster than labor wears.

—Noah Webster's 1828 Dictionary of American English

H6103 A feminine noun referring to laziness, sluggishness. It is a state and attitude of doing nothing; it destroys persons; and their possessions.

H6104 A feminine noun referring to idleness, sluggishness.

H7503 A verb meaning to become slack, to relax, to cease, to desist, to become discouraged, to become disheartened, to become weak, to become feeble, to let drop, to discourage, to leave alone, to let go, to forsake, to abandon, to be lazy. The word occurs forty-five times.

G3576 Slothful, sluggish, dull.

G3636 To be slow, to delay. Slow, tardy, slothful, lazy.

SUMMARY

Sloth is taking more from society or your family than you give back, either by not doing things at all or doing them poorly. "Day late—dollar short" is a common saying about this. So is "The Devil finds work for idle hands." One example is trading short-term gains for long-term losses by not being diligent at school. About sixty years ago, the U.S. Navy advertised for recruits by saying that they could retire by the age of thirty-eight. You can guess what type of people enlisted. I remember my late Naval NCO father describing how such people would not follow direct military orders and would complain that they were being oppressed and discriminated against when they were required to do their fair share of the work.

Being slothful causes harm in many ways. You will become despondent and moody. This will be followed by despair and finally by poverty. You will grow weary of life and suffer a premature death. This cause of death is common amongst retired people who do not keep active.

External symptoms are doing things with annoyance, resentment, slackness, and excuses. Negligence and carelessness are common symptoms. Internal ones are fear of failure resulting in failure to begin or accomplish something, or do good works. One of my mottos is, "Do not fail for lack of trying."

Finally, sloth will not withstand hard times.

SCRIPTURE ON SLOTH

Examples of Sloth

Proverbs 13:4: The soul of the sluggard craves and *gets* nothing, but the soul of the diligent is made fat.

Proverbs 26:13: The sluggard says, "There is a lion in the road! A lion is in the open square!"

14 *As* the door turns on its hinges, so *does* the sluggard on his bed.

15 The sluggard buries his hand in the dish; He is weary of bringing it to his mouth again.

16 The sluggard is wiser in his own eyes than seven men who can give a discreet answer.

Effects of Sloth

Proverbs 10:4: Poor is he who works with a negligent hand, but the hand of the diligent makes rich.

5 He who gathers in summer is a son who acts wisely, *but* he who sleeps in harvest is a son who acts shamefully.

Proverbs 15:19: The way of the lazy is as a hedge of thorns, but the path of the upright is a highway.

Proverbs 19:15: Laziness casts into a deep sleep, and an idle man will suffer hunger.

Proverbs 20:4: The sluggard does not plow after the autumn, so he begs during the harvest and has nothing.

Proverbs 21:25: The desire of the sluggard puts him to death, for his hands refuse to work;

26 All day long he is craving, while the righteous gives and does not hold back.

Proverbs 24:33: A little sleep, a little slumber, a little folding of the hands to rest,

34 Then your poverty will come *as* a robber and your want like an armed man.

Matthew Henry has observed:

Plutarch relates a saying of Cato Major: "That wise men profit more by fools than fools by wise men; for wise men will avoid the faults of fools, but fools will not imitate the virtues of wise men." Solomon reckoned that he *received instruction* by this sight, though it did not suggest to him any new notion or lesson, but only put him in mind of an observation he himself had formerly made, both of the ridiculous folly of the sluggard (who, when he has needful work to do, lies dozing in bed and cries, *Yet a little sleep, a little slumber;* and still it will be a little more, till he has slept his eyes out, and, instead of being fitted by sleep for business, as wise men are, he is dulled, and stupefied, and made good for nothing) and of certain misery that attends him: his *poverty comes as one that travels;* it is constantly coming nearer and nearer to him, and will be upon him speedily, and want seizes him as irresistibly *as an armed man,* a highwayman that will strip him of all he has. Now this is applicable, not only to our worldly business, to show what a scandalous thing slothfulness in that is, and how injurious to the family, but to the affairs of our souls. Note, (1.) Our souls are our fields and vineyards, which we are every one of us to take care of, to dress, and to keep. They are capable of being improved with good husbandry; that may be got out of them which will be fruit abounding to our account. We are charged with them, to occupy them till our Lord come; and a great deal of care and pains it is requisite that we should take about them. (2.) These fields and vineyards are often in a very bad state, not only no fruit brought forth, but all overgrown with *thorns* and *nettles* (scratching, stinging, inordinate lusts and passions, pride, covetousness, sensuality, malice, those are the thorns and nettles, the wild grapes, which the unsanctified heart produces), no guard kept against the enemy, but the *stone-wall broken down*, and all lies in common, all exposed. (3.) Where it is thus it is owing to the sinner's own slothfulness and folly. He is a sluggard, loves sleep, hates labour; and he is void of understanding, understands neither his business nor his interest; he is perfectly besotted. (4.) The issue of it will certainly be the ruin of the soul and all its welfare. It is everlasting want that thus comes upon it as an armed man. We know the place assigned to the wicked and slothful servant.

Condemnation of Sloth

Proverbs 10:26: Like vinegar to the teeth and smoke to the eyes, so is the lazy one to those who send him.

Proverbs 18:9: He also who is slack in his work Is brother to him who destroys.

CURES FOR SLOTH

As in all of the sins, you have to admit that you do it before you can do something about it. Get in touch with your motives. Pray when you start to have sloth. Enjoy doing a good job. Memorize some of the Scriptures above and say them to yourself. Print some on a card, then put in locations where you are most tempted.

Chaucer suggests practicing the following virtues: fortitude-strength, enduring patience and suffering, great well doing, and steadfastness-constancy.

Fortitude—Strength

FOR'TITUDE, n. [L. fortitudo, from fortis, strong.]

That strength or firmness of mind or soul, which enables a person to encounter danger with coolness and courage, or to bear pain or adversity without murmuring, depression or despondency. Fortitude is the basis or source of genuine courage or intrepidity in danger, of patience in suffering, of forbearance under injuries, and of magnanimity in all conditions of life. We sometimes confound the effect with the cause, and use fortitude as synonymous with courage or patience; but courage is an active virtue or vice, and patience is the effect of fortitude. Fortitude is the guard and support of the other virtues.

—Noah Webster's 1828 Dictionary of American English

Enduring patience and suffering

Hebrews 6:11: And we desire that each one of you show the same diligence so as to realize the full assurance of hope until the end, **12** so that you will not be sluggish, but imitators of those who through faith and patience inherit the promises.

Great well doing
Go out of your way to do a good job of it.

Steadfastness - Constancy
CONSTANCY, n. [L., to stand.]
1. Fixedness; a standing firm; hence, applied to God or his works, immutability; unalterable continuance; a permanent state.
2. Fixedness or firmness of mind; persevering resolution; steady, unshaken determination; particularly applicable to firmness of mind under sufferings, to steadiness in attachments, and to perseverance in enterprise. Lasting affection; stability in love or friendship.
3. Certainty; veracity; reality.

—Noah Webster's 1828 Dictionary of American English

I wrote this and my previous book in one or two hour periods each day. Throughout the day, I would get ideas. Then I would sit down at the computer, add a few sentences, and revise several others. In four months, each book was within 90 percent of the final form and in six months, it was 99 percent.

ADDITIONAL SCRIPTURE ON SLOTH:

Proverbs 6:6	Proverbs 12:27
Proverbs 19:15	Proverbs 20:13
Proverbs 21:5	Proverbs 22:13
Proverbs 23:21	Proverbs 28:19
Ecclesiastes 10:1	Ecclesiastes 11:6
Romans 12:10–11	2 Peter 1:5–11

Exercise 8. Write a paragraph about sloth and how it affects you. Include measures you will take to minimize it. Keep your results for use in exercise 9.

FINAL THOUGHTS

Exercise 9. Collect the paragraphs you wrote for the previous exercises and store them in a safe place. Every month review them and see if you are making progress in minimizing these sins in your life.

If you have gotten this far I hope that you have been provoked to think about your committing these sins and their seriousness, and take corrective measures. There is one more item. This involves attempting to flatter God into owing you favors. In England, this is called being a toady. Several hundred years ago, this was done by putting fur coats on statues of Mary. One modern example is adding extra titles to the name of each member of the Trinity as if "God" or "Jesus" was not enough of a lofty title by itself. Another common thing today is to try to curry favor with the second member of the Trinity by having the words of Jesus in red ink in their Bible.

2 Timothy 3:16: All Scripture is inspired by God and profitable for teaching, for reproof, for correction, for training in righteousness.

All Scripture is equally God's word. Red is also the worst possible color for causing reading fatigue. Keep the following verse always in your thoughts:

1 Samuel 15:22: Samuel said, "Has the LORD as much delight in burnt offerings and sacrifices as in obeying the voice of the LORD? Behold, to obey is better than sacrifice, *And* to heed than the fat of rams."

This involves the Old Covenant procedures of animal sacrifices. Translated into New Covenant language, it means that God is more pleased with your following His directions than He is with your going through ceremonial procedures, no matter how frequently or how elaborately done. The New Testament version is:

John 14:21: "He who has My command-ments and keeps them is the one who loves Me; and he who loves Me will be loved by My Father, and I will love him and will dis-close Myself to him."

Your life will experience trials and tribulations: spiritual, health and economic. The Bible has com-fort for theses.

Revelation 7:13: Then one of the elders answered, saying to me [John in heaven], "These who are clothed in the white robes, who are they, and where have they come from?"
14 I said to him, "My lord, you know." And he said to me, "These are the ones who come

out of the great tribulation, and they have washed their robes and made them white in the blood of the Lamb.

15 "For this reason, they are before the throne of God; and they serve Him day and night in His temple; and He who sits on the throne will spread His tabernacle over them."

I expect that in my lifetime there will be a drastic reduction in the standard of living caused by the rising demand for energy, food, and pure water causing everyone's share to decline and increase in price. I also expect to see outright religious persecutions. To be forewarned is to be forearmed. If you take the discussions on avarice and envy to heart, this diminution will not devastate you.

My final thought for you, the reader, is:

1 Corinthians 12:3: Therefore I make known to you that no one speaking by the Spirit of God says, "Jesus is accursed"; and no one can say, "Jesus is Lord," except by the Holy Spirit.

I pray that you can honestly say along with me:

JESUS IS LORD

REFERENCES

Original publication date, if known, is stated. Many of these books went through revisions and copyright extensions.

C. S. Lewis, *The Screwtape Letters*, Geoffrey Bliss, London, 1942

C. S. Lewis, *Mere Christianity*, Geoffrey Bliss, London, 1952

Matthew Henry, *A Commentary on the Whole Bible*, six volumes, Fleming H Revell Co., Old Tappan, NJ, no date

Dorothy L. Sayers, *Creed or Chaos?*, New York, Harcourt, Brace, 1949

Chaucer, Frank Ernest Hill (translator), *The Canterbury Tales*, London, Longman Green & Co., 1935

Gene Carpenter & Warren Baker (editors), *The Complete Word Study Dictionary: Old Testament*, AMG Publishers, 2005

Spiros Zodhiates & Warren Baker (editors), *The Complete Word Study Dictionary: New Testament*, AMG International, 1993